T0114934

Campground

Loretta Burns

Langaa Research & Publishing CIG
Mankon, Bamenda

Publisher:
Langaa RPCIG
Langaa Research & Publishing Common Initiative Group
P.O. Box 902 Mankon
Bamenda
North West Region
Cameroon
Langaagrp@gmail.com
www.langaa-rpcig.net

Distributed in and outside N. America by African Books Collective
orders@africanbookscollective.com
www.africanbookscollective.com

ISBN-10: 9956-764-90-6

ISBN-13: 978-9956-764-90-7

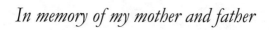

In memory of my mother and father

Table of Contents

I Poems..1

Principal...3
Beyond the Hyacinths.. 4
Curtains.. 5
Trochilidae.. 6
The Lady and the Dog.. 7
Five Pieces...8
Leavings...9
Assisted Living..11
Teacher, Teacher.. 12
Caretaker...14
Sawyerville.. 15
Villanelle No. 9... 17
The Times... 18
Fantasyman... 19
The Games...20
Suite of Rooms... 21
Woodfox...22
Pages... 23
MLK... 24
Master Charles...25
Campground.. 26
Paris...27
Greensboro Flower.. 29
1956...30
Two Ways...31
Woman from Ohio... 32
Edge of the Neighborhood................................ 33

Jekyll Island...34
On My Way to the P.O. 35
A Pretty Pleasure..37
Near the End of BO's Stretch....................39
Women of Color..40

II Fiction..41

To Walk in Jerusalem..................................43
Peach..49
The Crossing...59
Nothing Very New.......................................71

I

Oh, what a beautiful city . . .
—Traditional

Principal

My father
wore a fedora,
he looked like
the suited men
in *Look* and *Life*
only his skin
was papersack brown.

His father and his
grandfather,
once a slave,
put a bone in his back.

A ram's horn and
a fountain lived
in his throat,
and when he spoke
the people looked up.

A time of fear
but not for him.
He laughed but
did not smile or
play.

Beyond the Hyacinths

Two of the eagles,
the ones in the cage,
had mated,
rejecting the third,
who perched like a Buddha
beyond the box.

His wings clipped,
he could only dream
of cliffs
and white water.

The little family paused,
the youngster's eyes
fixed first on the pair
and then the stranger.

The scene was no
colder than what
might have been,
but I walked slower
as I exited
that placid ground,
facing the road and sky,
so rough, so ready.

Curtains

Miss Mandy used to
tell the three children
she minded that when
she was younger all the
white ladies in town
would bring her their
curtains to wash, starch,
stretch, and iron.
It took hours she said
to get them just right,
two dollars for each pair.
One day after she had
done Miss Myrtle's bunch
and folded and piled them
just so on the bed,
the cat went and
did his business
all over the fluffy pink.
Miss Mandy had to
start all over but not
before she caught
the cat and chopped
off his head.

Trochilidae

By day
the hummingbird
must feed
every quarter hour.
At night
it goes into a torpor,
unable to move,
exposed to passing
snakes, giant mantises
and hawks.
Imagine its relief
on waking.
Alive to seek the
bee balm and columbine,
Chinese lantern and
honeysuckle,
sage and water willow,
firebrush and fuchsia.
Night is an illusion,
this only is real,
this only is real,
this only is real.

The Lady and the Dog

Beside the preacher's
Spanish house lived a
lady with a beautiful dog.
His hair was yellow
and soft and long
and he was always
ready to run.
The lady left her
quiet husband almost
once a year.
He took up with others
but only until she came back
and drove them out.
The children liked
the pretty woman
but always wondered why
when she left she never took
her beautiful dog,
to sit by her in the daytime
and walk her all the way
home at night.

Five Pieces

Before the census taker knocked,
the mother took the bread
from the pan and broke it
in five pieces.
Meal and water,
baking powder and salt,
a little oil made
five brown pieces
to end the day.
When the knock came,
the young ones—four—
were already at table.
He asked what he had
come to ask, noting silently
the sadness of
everything in the room,
except the five pieces
and her gaze on the four.
He left, having taken
their measure, lingering
for a heartbeat
outside the door.

Leavings

Heading out
for new territory,
a night departure
is right.
A midnight plane,
an evening train,
or even a
late greyhound.
The boy who quit
his Southern town
to join his ace
in the Paris needle
must surely have felt
that cape of dark,
a quiver he could
never name.
The harbor lights
told the woman
in blue that she was
hardly the first or last.
The put-upon wife under
the street lamp waiting
for someone to
drive her out of town.

Homecoming
requires a morning move,
as brisk and clean as
a surgeon's blade.
Decline politely

invitations to lunch,
have bags at the ready
if waiting for news,
and when it comes
go swiftly out.
If travelling by car
drive sure and
straight through.
If night catches you
you're not to worry,
you left in the morning,
and in the clear.

Assisted Living

The neighbor,
a respectable, Republican
lady, went quietly,
thinking she would
come back soon.
The two daughters and the
son were blameless and
so were the salamanders
that climbed the bricks
in June, July and August.
A granddaughter, newly
wed, and her groom
would take the house.
And so the lady went
to a pleasant place
not far from the edge of town.
A man from her church
had gone before and right
glad he was to be there.
It had to be all right, they said,
the best thing—the only thing.
And who would quibble
when they saw
her crock pot and hydrangea
waiting soundlessly
by the curb?

Teacher, Teacher

He owned a car
and drove from the
neighboring county
on Sunday evenings.
They sat in the small
parlor in winter
and out on the porch
in spring.
They talked of school
and what they would
do in the summertime
back at their homes.
Sometimes they
walked down the road
and back.
She told him how
she had to go fishing
with her landlady—not
wanting to stay in the
house alone—and how
she shivered when she
heard the sound the
moccasins made as they
slid from the bank
into the water.
He told her next year
He might move to
a little bigger town.
The man he boarded with
said country people had

peculiar ways and were
sometimes hard to teach,
told him he was on a slow train
and better look out for himself.
She said she always had
company when she walked
through a stretch of dark woods,
and she could barely pack
all the jelly jars that covered
her desk last May.

Caretaker

Polk would doubtless
have taken his picture,
freezing the onyx skin,
white beard and mane,
eloquent eyes in a face
of quiet care,
a carriage no one might
purchase.
He tended the graveyard
next to the painted-blue church,
working late on
moon-bright nights,
perhaps to escape the heat,
always singing as he
swung his sling blade.
His voice rising from the
quiet dark—more like
the Crescent's wail than the
whippoorwill's yodel about
the chip and the white oak—
could be heard for miles.
Was he afraid of the yard
at that hour?
Was he appeasing the dead
for stealing their time?
Was his song a kindred
cry to those who listen
for night sounds,
unable to close their eyes?

Sawyerville

Something always bloomed
splendidly in Cousin Anne's
front yard, no matter
the time of year.
Unlike Uncle William's sturdy
castle across the road with
its tidy moat of green,
mostly cactus and elephant ear,
Cousin Anne's reds, whites,
yellows and blues whispered
chants when the wind blew,
carrying them far off
to the butterflies and bees,
which appeared like empty
pitchers before the fountains
of flower head,
tarrying till sundown
and flying heavily
drifting off.
And when one day we
spied the hummingbird—
the first we had seen
with naked eye—
floating over the foxgloves,
kissing the columbines,
we knew a Sunday joy
and understood that Cousin Anne
was once upon a time.
When all her children moved away
Anne stayed behind almost alone

to watch over and walk
her favored ground.

Villanelle No. 9

The mystery of the light I cannot know,
its ecstasies I feel in every vein,
I chase the light until I have to go.

The green trees lean their branches deep and low,
a soothing sight outside my windowpane,
the mystery of the light I cannot know.

Each day is still a marvel fast or slow,
a city street or any muted plain,
I chase the light until I have to go.

I know about the promise of the bow,
and all we must endure of loss and pain,
the mystery of the light I cannot know.

The earth is filled with travelers by the row,
of those who stir the tea and cut the cane,
I chase the light until I have to go.

I do not fear the chill of winter's snow,
I glory in the wash of summer rain,
the mystery of the light I cannot know,
I chase the light until I have to go.

The Times

Always they acknowledge him,
the ones with letters covered
in leaves and stone.
They mean to be kind.
Anxiously he waits his turn,
his beard and garb unchanged.
So is his text but he can still
upset the people.
When he is done they
stand and stomp and clap
as if they are ready.
He rides
these perfect minutes.
When all is over
he goes home to wait
for the apocalypse,
or the next conference call.

Fantasyman

It's nearly always
the City
that conjures him.
Its eccentric
blue-black rhythms,
muted two a.m.
avenues after rain
and no moon,
a fade-in duet
by lamplight,
a silky Roy Ayers and
"Don'tcha Say No."
He is very fine.
He comes, not only
when she calls,
but unbidden—
unexpected
like April snows
he shakes her
from quotidian care,
retells her stories,
fills her bowl
to overflowing.
Her conspirator,
she will
abandon him
heedlessly.
He will not
let her go.

The Games

Against reason
and nature's code,
fierce beauty panting
for fragments of time.
Pain is their true
companion.
Behold them,
hard and radiant
they launch,
grimacing and
waving at death
with one finger.

Suite of Rooms

Patiently
we wait our turn,
chatting with the
other who came
if we're lucky.
If not,
reading—maybe—
or trying to look
casual.
We don't complain
about the wait,
the musty magazines,
the wrong channel,
the strong soap
in the bathroom.
We are the humble,
the meek.
They have something
we want.
We will wait
all day to hear
those dull and
dulcet refrains,
the ones we pray for
and commit to memory.
The mantra we like
almost best is
"Come back
in a year."

Woodfox

Angola
forty years
isolation.

Does your soul
look back and wonder?
Do you hum Mahalia's
song when you
wake at night?

What song did you
hum in the abyss?
Was it "I believe
I'll run on"?

Do not fret that
you swallowed
the lure to freedom.

You are
the wood fox,
the improviser,
the dreamer.
You know
they know
you cannot be caught.

Pages

Secrets not shared
with comrades or kin,
they write.
Do they trust
someone like me,
or am I the anonymous
confessional in the
strange city?
Without guile
they cannot know
the cost of knowing
the lecherous stepfather,
the T-cell count,
the imminent termination.
They cannot know and
must forgive me for the
blood on the sheet.

MLK

Martin Luther King
spoke
at my college
graduation.
It was outside
in the open air
on a sweltering
May day
in Alabama.
Three years
later
he died
on my birthday.
We were having
a party
when the news
came.
Later that
evening,
to splinter the
panes of silence,
someone
put on a record.
It was Aretha
Franklin singing
"Ain't no way
for me to love you
if you won't
let me."

Master Charles

When he was young
and I was younger
Julian Bond wrote
a poem about you.
Now Julian's gone
and you've rolled on.
Still the doctor's got
medicine and money,
the avenue's lonely,
the night time's
the right time,
and the dreaming woman
calls for Johnny,
when she knows
your name is Ray.

Campground

Nature was ours,
our eldest elders named it.
Marauding barefoot
through Johnson grass
and rabbit tobacco
ready to be amazed—
like the time we looked
up and saw the martin
attacking the hawk.
We captured snake
doctors and devil
horses and chased after
shimmering eyes
in the blue of night.
Mystery and wildness
beckoned and were
not dreadful.
We remade the world and
filled our jugs with it,
unmindful that never
would we sense again
such naked force coursing
through our quick and
lovely veins.

Paris

The two Jewish girls
and I were savoring the
Sorbonne for a year.
One was a Kim Novak
look-alike from Indiana,
the other a smart brassy
blond from Manhattan.
We lived in a five-story
walk-up and I could see
Notre Dame from my window.
We called the owner's
wife Madame Defarge but
we liked the maid, Louise,
and the porter, Monsieur Duval.
On Thursday nights, for a
change, we ate at the Italian
restaurant up the street,
ordering the "young girl's
dream" for dessert.
These were fine times,
living outside the annals.
Then, shortly before the
invasion of Cambodia,
the brassy blond was
arrested for holding a joint.
Released, she left before year's
end to avoid the court date.
Kim Novak was brought up
short and realized that
April was ending,

and I remembered.

Greensboro Flower

The angel's trumpet
in its shocking splendor
poses a question and
answers with itself,
its image in canvas and
song a rich conversion—
neither as ineffably
beautiful as the fledgling
girl beside the bloom,
smiling for a picture.

1956

Passing through
Montgomery during
the bus boycott,
we saw a woman
walking.
My mother told
my father to stop,
but at that moment
the car in front
of him pulled over
and the woman got in.
My father said there
was no need to hurry
home—we were only
eighty miles away—and
my mother agreed.

Two Ways

She took him to the park
to walk beside the lake
and look at the ducks.
He was from another land.
The next night he and a friend
caught one of the ducks,
took it home in a sack,
killed it
picked it
cooked it
and ate it.

Woman from Ohio

The male hippopotamus
flings his dung with his tail
to warn intruders.
This is an unlovely sight,
even on a screen,
but to an alien visitor—
or a child—might seem
as enchanting as forsythia
in bloom or the demoiselle
crane in flight.

One September day
a woman from Ohio
looked out of a car
window and gushed
about the beauty of the
Alabama cotton fields.

Edge of the Neighborhood

Sometimes the paper
comes late and
sometimes not at all,
but I walk outside
each morning—always
startled by the miracle
of wakening—to make certain
the street, the houses,
the trees, the sky
have not disappeared
during the night.
Assured I am not
in the zone,
I linger to regard the
hawthorns and nandinas
that tend themselves,
and listen for
sunrise sounds,
this slender ritual my
thanksgiving
for breathing
the imperfect air.

Jekyll Island

Rehabilitated,
the sea turtle was
dropped at the edge
of the ocean but
would not go in.
The young coats
had no choice but
to take her back—
to the small pool
in the clinic,
to fish trapped in
ice blocks,
to play periods
and enemas
when necessary.
Who needs
the great wide waters,
the long trudge to the beach,
the wearisome
depositing of eggs,
the miserable crawl
back out to sea?

On My Way to the P.O.

On my way to the P.O.
Stevie Wonder's "As"—
also known as
"I'll Be Loving You Always"—
came on the radio.
It had been awhile so
I turned up the volume.
When they hit the
second call-response
groove I was almost there,
but Stevie's "alwaaays"
and the moaning
of the back-up singers
behind the keyboard
sent me into a half-trance
like the first time.
I left my body to
dance in the clearing
under the ocher moon
with the others.
When I pulled
into the parking lot
they were still driving,
and I had to wait
till they were done
and catch my breath
before leaving the car
and walking
through the door,
pretending it was

just another day.

A Pretty Pleasure

At dusk
before the moonflowers opened,
we sat on the ground cross-legged
awaiting their display.
The aunts and older cousins
stayed inside or on the porch,
except for Rachel,
who was in between.
She watched with us.

Purple and white
the flowers grew up high
on vines and row by row.
Closed up by day, at sundown
they were wanton, spreading their
petal horns slowly before our
raptured eyes to a ritual music
we could almost hear.

It was sheltered magic—
honeyed, not cold.

When finally we came inside,
washed our bodies and
went to bed,
I dreamed of the flowers
blooming in the dark,
dreamed and wondered
was nothing left there watching
except the moon.

Near the End of BO's Stretch

The face
no longer new,
the heart
beneath the arc,
the soul
a truer witness.

The stride
unchanged—
no shuffle there—
its message in
each step.

He is still
and always
in the house
and in the mind.

A son of the brave
and the babes
in the street,
a vanquisher
for the road
and for the books,
a lovely
promise piece,
a dream wedge.

Women of Color

Family legend avows that
great-great grandmother Bay
attacked an overseer
who was whipping her boy.

Great-grandmother Melinda
hummed sorrowful songs
that hung about the
heart like gemstone.

Grandmother Frances
told haunting stories
of journeys, stations,
and trains.

My mother
taught all her students
how to leap
like gazelles.

II

Big star's falling,
I know it can't be long before day.
  —Traditional

To Walk in Jerusalem

Before Charlie James Patterson was called to preach, he had been a fairly ordinary boy, on the surface at least. The only things that distinguished him at all were his fragile good looks. He had a slender, graceful figure, beautiful copper-colored skin, and, according to his grandmother, "the prettiest eyes God ever made." In other ways, however, he was a boy much like any other in Reed Station, Alabama. But at the age of seventeen he had a dream in which the Lord told him to carry His word to the people.

Before this, Charlie James had been an indifferent member of his grandmother's church—the True Deliverance House of Prayer—since he was fourteen. In fact, in his younger days he had been a little ashamed of attending a sanctified church when most of his buddies and their families attended the Baptist church. Sometimes his friends would accompany him to night services to pat their feet to the drums and tambourines, to giggle at the fat sisters who danced in the aisle, and to stare, spellbound at times, at the ones who spoke in tongues. On these occasions Charlie James made a special effort to appear detached from the goings on, as indeed he was.

He had joined the church in the first place because of a nightmare. When he was thirteen, his grandmother, Miss Edna, had started warning him of the peril his soul was in. He would have joined then, just to stop her sermonizing—it meant that little to him—but it was not a simple matter to join the chosen of True Deliverance. One had to have a vision, a sign that one was ready to be saved, so Charlie James had to tarry in the wilderness before crossing over. Miss Edna counseled him to watch and pray.

He prayed but little and watched not at all, and his sign did not come. One night, however, he had a nightmare about being lost in a swamp and being rescued by his father, whom he had never seen. Miss Edna said that the swamp stood for hell and the "father" who rescued him was his heavenly father. She then dropped to her knees and praised the Lord for saving her child. Since this dream qualified as a true vision, she told Charlie James that he was ready to become a member of the fold. He joined the church at the next service, was baptized a week later and his grandmother left him, more or less, in peace. When his mother, who lived in Detroit, learned of his conversion, she wrote him a letter asking him to pray for her.

Charlie James himself felt no change, and his life went on much as before. He still did not shout or dance or speak in tongues, and when other church members, especially those his own age, exhibited these behaviors, he was mystified. A girl named Irene told him that he might be saved but that he was still not sufficiently sanctified with the Holy Ghost. She was forever saying to him, "Charlie James, your light ain't shinin'."

His light remained hidden until the fourth month of his seventeenth year, when he was chosen by God. It was late October 1952. Charlie James had been hunting that day, and his favorite dog had been bitten by a snake and had died. That night, while he slept, a figure appeared to him in a brilliant light and said, "Take my message to the people." When Charlie James asked, "What if they don't believe me?" the figure answered, "Those who do not believe shall be damned." Charlie James had awakened sweating and shaken, convinced that he had been called to preach. When he told his dream to Miss Edna, she questioned him thoroughly for over an hour. Then, after she was satisfied, she said that he must proclaim his revelation.

From that day, Charlie James was a changed man. He went from door to door, telling neighbors and friends of his call. He declared himself to the flock at True Deliverance, and since they were without a regular pastor, offered himself as their spiritual leader. There was great jubilation that day as the church drew him to its bosom, and shouts of "Praise the Lord" and "Help him Jesus" resonated throughout the sanctuary. Most church members were surprised by the young man's divine summons, but his grandmother said she had always known he would be something special because of his tender heart.

Charlie James was nervous and shy at first in his new role, but after hitting his stride he became a skillful preacher. He had a strong voice and could speak the word. He could sing and was good-looking. And it was not long before he discovered that he, too, had the gift of tongues.

The ways of the saints—as they were called somewhat derisively by others—was not an easy one. They did not smoke or drink or listen to barrelhouse music, and the women wore no powder or paint. They believed that one had to be ever vigilant in the struggle against the devil's wiles, and to that end sinners among them were pointed out and admonished. If the offense was severe enough, transgressors could be put out of the church until they repented. At each service a time was set aside for the laying on of hands—not to anoint or heal, but to accuse. If a member knew that someone had sinned, it was that member's duty to lay hands on the offender so that the sin might be revealed and corrected. Sins of the flesh were a special abomination. Annabelle Brooks had laid hands on her own daughter for the sin of fornication, and Hazel Brooks had to quit the church until after her child was born. She then had to confess her sin publicly and ask God's—and the church's—

forgiveness to be reinstated. The laying on of hands in this way had never concerned Charlie James before, but it troubled him at the beginning of his ministry. When he witnessed the sorrowful tears, the downcast eyes, the shame and torment of the accused, he felt sorry. It was hard to regard them as tools of the devil. Eventually, though, he came to view the ritual as necessary to the salvation of those who had strayed. It was painful, but the reward was repentance and freedom from sin.

A little over a year after Charlie James had received his call, Della Mae Silman rose from her seat one Sunday morning to announce that the Lord had spoken to her in a dream and had told her to marry "our anointed pastor." Charlie James was struck dumb. Della Mae was pushing forty, had a twenty-one year old daughter, and was exceedingly plain. Miss Edna could hardly contain herself. She had never cared for Della Mae, and now the thought of this middle-aged clinker top trying to force herself on Charlie James nearly made the old lady forget where she was. She boldly challenged Della Mae's dream and said it must have been a message from the devil. Della Mae, arms akimbo, insisted that it was a divine vision that must be obeyed.

"I know what the Lord done told me, you don't."

"I know the Lord and nobody else ain't told you to marry my child."

"You better watch out old woman. You messin' with God."

Brother Winston tried to keep the peace—"Now ladies— please—remember, we in the house of the Lord"—but he was silenced by the two women. Other members of the congregation became embroiled in the argument, shouting one another down. Charlie James, after recovering himself as best he could, interceded and promised that he would pray for guidance.

He agonized for weeks over Della Mae's announcement. His grandmother pleaded with him to pay it no heed, and Charlie James surely did not want to marry Della Mae. But it was this fact that, in the end, convinced him that he should do so. This was a test of his faith. The Lord was trying him, and if he should scorn Della Mae's sign, he would be found wanting. It was therefore his duty as the Lord's messenger to do as the Lord had bidden.

So Charlie James and Della Mae were married.

Charlie James left his grandmother's house, the only home he had known, and moved in with Della Mae and her daughter, Ruby Nell. In the beginning, Della Mae, in her youngest dreams, could not have wished for a kinder, more solicitous, more tolerant husband. He had said to her on the day they got married, "I mean to make you a good husband, Della Mae." And she had answered, "I know you do, Rev'end." He prayed constantly for strength and guidance, and Della Mae, too, was doing her part. By marrying Charlie James she had incurred the wrath, not only of Miss Edna, but of most of the other women in the church, who were convinced she had tricked him and taken advantage of his sincerity and his youth. But Della Mae did not flaunt her victory. In fact, after the marriage she assumed a demeanor that was uncharacteristically humble. She became quiet and soft-spoken. The changes in her were sufficiently striking that a few of the women began to consider the possibility that the vision was indeed genuine. In her relationship with Charlie James, Della Mae was an adoring helpmate, struggling to make up in devotion and generosity of spirit for what she lacked in youth and allure.

But as time passed, there were indications that all was not well with the reverend. Charlie James's sermons began to take on a rambling quality, and his speech became halting. He still maintained a presence in the pulpit, but he seemed to lose some of his fire. His young face began to look haggard, his eyes, distressed. Always a careful dresser, he started to appear slightly rumpled, almost unkempt. Church members whispered among themselves and prayed in their hearts that his tribulation would pass and he would come out the other side. Della Mae, for her part, retreated behind an unrevealing mask and put it all in the hands of the Lord. Miss Edna, reasoning that Charlie James's marriage to Della Mae was the cause of his torment, begged him to free himself. But in time, after the other gossip began, she could only suffer for him. Sunday after Sunday, Charlie James looked out at his congregation with a face and eyes that were at first eager and strained, then desperate and pleading—like someone caught in the middle of a rising stream.

When he and Della Mae had been married almost a year and a half, Della Mae's daughter, Ruby Nell, stopped coming to church. Four months later she gave birth to a baby boy and named him Curtis. On the first Sunday after Ruby Nell's child was born, Charlie James preached a passionate sermon on the death of Ishbaal, one of Saul's sons. After he finished, he walked from the pulpit and out the door, and did not come back to True Deliverance until six years later, when his body was brought home from Detroit for burial. It was said he drank himself to death.

Peach

It was Thursday night, and Luther was hurrying to dress and get over to Earlene's house. He had been late getting home from work and had barely had time to take a bath. He never knew what mood she might be in, and he worried that she might not let him in if he wasn't on time. Although he bought her gifts and gave her money—always money—he had, on more than one occasion, seen her open the door, take what he had brought, and close the door in his face. He looked in the mirror to check his clothes, grabbed his car keys, and headed out.

As he drove the few miles to Earlene's, he thought about the last time he had been with her. She had been mighty sweet to him that night, and he had stayed almost until morning. His family—his mother and his sisters—thought he was crazy for fooling with someone like her. She saw other men and took their money, too. She wasn't a prostitute—exactly—but she would not give a man the time of day if he couldn't—or wouldn't—bring her money. She cared nothing for Luther, they said, and maybe they were right. He hated the thought of her seeing other men, but from the time she had smiled at him at the Labor Day fish fry, he had been hooked. He had never let a woman spin him around before, but he couldn't seem to help himself when it came to her. He could hardly wait for Thursday night, his night, and he tried to put out of his mind the other nights of the week at her house.

Luther was not bad looking, but he was by no means a ladies' man. When he was eighteen, he fell in love with a girl named Lois, but they had split up, and she had married someone else. He went with a few women after that, but no one held him until Earlene. She was so—out of the ordinary. She smoked cigarettes on the street, treated men the way men treated women, and didn't care what people thought. More than that, she didn't seem to look down on herself the way the barrelhouse women did. He was almost as taken with how she carried herself as he was with her looks, which rivaled those of some of the beauties in Ebony magazine, so Luther thought.

All the men he knew, young and old, agreed that Earlene was the second best-looking woman in town—the best-looking woman being Sally Flakes, the undertaker's wife. The women acknowledged, grudgingly, that Earlene was nice-looking, then disparaged her for the way she lived, but that didn't keep her from going to church—when she took a notion—always wearing a bright-colored dress and wide hat and sitting on or near the front row. She was thirty-two but could pass, she said, for twenty-five. She had no regular job and when she wasn't working spent most of her days listening to the radio, sitting on her porch—weather permitting—walking back and forth to the store, or visiting her friend Alberta, who was also home all day but earned money by dressing hair in her kitchen. One man or another came to Earlene's house three or four nights a week, and if on a given evening she did not feel like being bothered—or sharing her bed—she told the man, "Come back next week." But no one came on Monday. On Monday nights she and Alberta went to Camp's, a café and juke joint nearby, where they ate, drank, and danced until midnight.

Luther pulled up to her house at ten minutes after eight, got out of the car, and knocked on the door. He waited, then knocked again. Earlene came to the door dressed in a housecoat and let him come in.

"You was about to be late."

"I was late getting off work."

"Well, I'm not feeling good. I'm going back to bed."

"OK."

Luther was very disappointed but tried not to show it. He wanted to sit down at least, but Earlene did not move from the door. They stood for a moment, Earlene taking a handkerchief from her housecoat pocket and wiping her nose, before Luther took out his wallet and gave her a twenty-dollar bill.

"Can you sit and talk for a minute?"

"No. I told you I'm sick. You can take me to the picture show next week."

Earlene opened the door for Luther to depart.

"I'll see you Thursday," he said, as he left, but before he reached his car, Earlene called to him.

"Bring me a half-gallon of peach ice cream. *Peach.* Don't bring me no pint-size, hear? You can keep the pint-size. I want a full half-gallon."

"A half-gallon of peach. OK."

Luther drove home, washed the dishes he had left in the sink, and went to bed. He went to work the next day and spent Saturday working in his mother's yard and painting her fence. He picked her up Sunday morning, and they both went to church, staying for the youth program after the regular service. He meant to get the half-gallon of peach ice cream on Monday, but he worked double shifts at the mill. The foreman had asked him to do the same for the rest of the week, but Luther told him Tuesday and Friday were the only other days he could work two shifts back to back.

As soon as Luther got off work on Wednesday, he went straight to Mr. Thompson's store, about two miles from the mill, to see if they had the ice cream. Thompson's had half-gallons of chocolate, vanilla, and strawberry but no peach. He then tried the Hancocks' store down the road from Thompson's, but they didn't have it either. He drove to town next and tried A. & P. and Piggly Wiggly. A. & P. had a pint-sized container of peach but no half-gallon. Luther, who did not eat sweets because of his diabetes, had not realized that a half-gallon of peach ice cream would be so hard to find. He didn't dare show up at Earlene's without it, so he decided to drive over to Greenville and check the stores there before they closed.

He drove the seventeen miles to Greenville and searched in their A. & P., Kroger, and Colonial, but neither store had a half-gallon of peach. He was frustrated and annoyed. The trip had been for nothing.

About half way home, he started thinking about what he would say to Earlene the next evening and what he might buy her to make up for the ice cream. Not getting what she asked for would put her in an evil frame of mind, and she might send him away again. Before he could finish this thought, he heard a loud noise like a gun shot and felt his car lurch to one side. He slowed down, pulled over to the side of the road and got out. He had had a blow out—the tire on the front right side was ruined. Worse than that, he had no spare—he had given it to his nephew James who needed it for his car. He had meant to replace the spare but had kept putting it off. He was still around ten miles from home with nothing in between, and besides, it was after six o'clock, and everything would be closed anyway. He would have to walk home, buy a tire the next day, and get somebody to bring him back to his car. Luther drew a deep breath, locked his car, and started walking. Maybe a colored person would pick him up. There's always something, he thought.

More than a few cars with white drivers passed him, but when he had walked for about forty-five minutes, he heard a car behind him slowing down. As it pulled alongside him, Luther looked up and saw that the driver was not only colored but someone he knew—Ike Chambers.

"Hey, man. Is that your car back there?"

"Yeah. I had a blow out."

"No spare?"

"Naw."

"Hop in"

Luther had hoped to hitch a ride home, but why did it have to be Ike Chambers who happened by? He was one of Earlene's other men friends. After a moment's hesitation, Luther jumped in the car.

The two men were silent for the first few minutes of the ride, and the only sound was the automobile's hum. Luther felt awkward and embarrassed. It was bad enough that he had to accept help from a rival, but Ike was dressed in a smart-looking blue shirt and striped pants that looked brand new. Luther had on his work clothes—overalls—and felt dusty and smelly.

Finally, Ike said, "Lucky I came along, huh?" Luther nodded.

Ike was a guy it was hard not to like, and if not for Earlene, Luther would have liked him. He wasn't a particularly handsome man, but he had a relaxed, self-assured manner that appealed to women and impressed other men. He also talked better than most people in Luther's circle of friends. He didn't have a lot more education than Luther, who had dropped out of school after the eleventh grade, but to hear Ike talk you might think he had been to college. His job was also different. Most men—and all of Luther's friends and acquaintances—

worked in the textile mills that dominated the small villages in that part of the state, but Ike worked at Epstein's, the music store downtown. He was a handyman when he first started, but eventually, aside from his other duties, he was permitted to wait on the Negro customers and collect the money from Mr. Epstein's juke boxes around the county. This was unusual for the Deep South of the 1950s, and it gave him a status above that of most colored working men.

Luther had heard one of his sisters say that Ike was the only man Earlene didn't lead around by the nose. He wondered if Ike knew about *him*. He was glad it was going to be a short ride.

"So what's been going on?" Ike said.

"Nothing much. Just working every day."

"What shift are you on now?"

"First shift."

"You like first shift?"

"It's fine. I don't like second shift. Third shift is all right."

"I tried the mills when I was a boy, but I didn't stay long. That's some rough work."

"Yeah, it's rough, but you got to have a paycheck."

"I hear you. But did you ever notice how many people get sick around here?"

"People get sick everywhere."

"I know, but breathing in that cotton dust can't be good."

Luther paused. He breathed in cotton dust all day, five—sometimes six—days a week. It filled the air like snow.

"You might be right, but like I said, you got to have a paycheck," he said.

"Do you wear something over your nose and mouth when you're working?"

"Me? Naw."

"It might keep you from messing up your lungs."

A few of the men where Luther worked wore handkerchiefs or bandanas over their faces, but Luther never did. He had worked in the mills since he was seventeen and had never thought about it. He was twenty-eight years old—in his prime. Older people got messed-up lungs, cancer, and things like that, didn't they? That's the way life went, and what could you do about it?

"Ain't no scarf can keep off sickness and death," he said.

"Maybe it won't, but it might help. What do you have to lose?"

"I don't know. Nothing, I guess."

"It's a shame people have to work in these mills to earn a living. No union. Nobody to look out for you."

"Bossmen always talking against the union."

"What do you expect? No union, they do what they want."

By now, they had passed the town limit and had reached Chester Road.

"You live over in Ames Alley, don't you?"

"Right."

When they reached Ames Alley, Luther directed Ike to his house, and Ike pulled over. Luther got out of the car, closed the door, and leaned in the window.

"Thanks, man. I appreciate it."

"Do you have a way to get back to your car tomorrow?"

"I'll get one of my buddies to take me—after I get a tire."

"Better get two. One to put on and a spare."

"Right. Take it easy."

"You too, man."

Ike drove off, and Luther entered his house. He hadn't eaten since lunch and was hungry. He fixed himself a sandwich and a Coke and then walked down the rows of rented mill

55

houses until he came to his friend Jerome's door. He told Jerome he needed a ride to work in the morning. That was no problem since Luther and Jerome worked the same shift at the same mill. He also needed to buy a tire and pick up his car. They agreed that Jerome would pick Luther up in the morning and take him to work. At lunchtime they would go to the bank and after work to Ingram's to purchase the tire—Luther would have to wait until payday to buy a spare—and Jerome would take him to his car.

Next day, by the time Luther had picked up his car and driven back home, it was after eight. He grabbed a bite to eat, took a bath—as he always did on Thursday—got dressed, and drove over to Earlene's. He got there around nine.

He knocked three times before she came to the door and let him in. She was made up and dressed to go out, but her face was fixed in a rigid scowl.

"You know what time it is?

"I had a flat yesterday coming from Greenville. I didn't have a spare and had to leave the car. I went back today to get it and just got back."

Earlene relaxed her face only a little and walked over to the sofa. Luther followed, and they both sat down. Only then did Earlene notice that he was empty-handed.

"Where is my peach ice cream?

"I couldn't find a half-gallon of peach. I looked but I couldn't find it."

"Couldn't find it? I bet you didn't half look."

"I looked. I didn't find anything but a pint-size, and you said don't bring that. I even drove over to Greenville.

"I been tuned up all day for my peach ice cream, and you come in here talking about you couldn't find it. Men ain't good for nothing."

Luther looked down at the floor, and his eyes strayed over to her shoes. She had on black pumps that were slightly misshapen because of the bunions on her feet.

"It's too late to go to the picture show," he said. You want to listen to the radio?"

"No."

"You want to play some cards?"

"I don't feel like playing cards."

"You got any beer? I can go pick some up."

"I don't want to drink no beer."

Luther was not surprised by her attitude—he had expected worse—but he *was* surprised by his response.

"Well, if you don't feel like doing anything, I guess I'll get on back home. I got to work double shifts tomorrow."

Earlene looked at him out of the corner of her eye.

"Suit yourself," she said.

Luther got up and Earlene followed him to the door. When he opened the door and turned to face her, he encountered the expectant look he had come to know well.

"I'm low on money this week," he said. "I had to buy a tire."

"What's that got to do with me?"

"I don't have nothing to give you."

"Nothing?"

Luther shook his head.

"First, you don't have my peach ice cream, and now you telling me you don't have no money. You a sorry sight this evening."

"I'll see you," Luther said.

"Maybe you will and maybe you won't."

"I'll see you," Luther repeated, and walked through the door.

The Crossing

Geneva got up at daybreak and lit the green candle she kept on the mantel. She had to hurry because her Aunt Pearlie would be rising in another half hour. She slipped a dress on over her nightgown, tied a scarf around her head, and put on the brogan shoes she used for work. She removed five dollar bills from underneath the mattress and put them in the pocket of her dress. A cloth panel that hung to the floor separated the two bedrooms in the house, and Geneva was relieved when she pulled it to one side and saw her aunt's bed cover being lifted up and down by deep, measured breaths. She blew out the candle and walked back to the kitchen where she could see by the light from the double windows. She dipped some water from the bucket on the wooden stand and walked out on the back porch, rinsed her mouth with the water, and spat it out over the edge of the porch. As she walked back inside to return the dipper to the bucket, she heard Miss Artelia's rooster crow.

She went down the back steps and across the yard in the direction of the large fig tree to the right. She walked through the opening between the chicken house and the well, rounded the outhouse, went through the gate, and started crossing the pasture on the other side of the fence. The cow was grazing at the far left end that was not visible from the house. When she came to the fence on the other side of the pasture, she eased her body in between the strings of barbed wire and walked in between two shotgun houses and across a dirt road to reach another field. This one was wider and would take longer to cross. As she trudged through the tall, wet grass and dandelion weeds, she studied on what she was about to do.

Geneva could not remember when the thought had first occurred to her. Perhaps it had begun as a vague, ill-formed notion in some region of her mind and had grown, little by little, to a clear, sharply focused plan—she didn't know. But after she had become fully aware of the idea, it was never out of her head. And now she had decided to act. Like a wounded pilgrim on her way to bathe in holy waters, she was struggling, daring to believe.

She thought of John Allen's sturdy brown shoulders—his wayward smile and clean, white teeth. She despised him.

Geneva was only sixteen, but already she had known a woman's torment. Miss Pearlie had warned her, but she had gone her own way.

John Allen had been her first real boyfriend. No one had ever said she was pretty, but she had large, light-brown eyes, and the bones in her pecan-colored face were strong and well defined. Miss Lillian, who lived down by the depot and sold whiskey, had told her once, "You ain't the cutest, but you got sump'm."

John Allen had wild ways, but this tended to make him more beguiling. After he had come back from Korea, got a job at the packing house, and bought a car, he was—as he himself put it—"all the young girls' fret." And even the good sisters who shook their heads and grunted when his name was mentioned had to admit that he was "built up real good." But it wasn't just his looks that were appealing. He exuded a disarming boyishness that the army had not destroyed and that both women and men found hard to resist. Geneva could not believe it when he began to notice her. When he asked if he could come to see her, she told him she would have to ask her Aunt Pearl. Miss Pearlie had been adamant. She had said, "He too old, and he don't mean you no good. You want to end up rockin' a baby? What you look like, carryin' on with somebody twenty-five years old?" But the girl's nagging and pleading had worn her down. Geneva was almost a woman and not as easy to rule as before. So after lengthy talks and prayer, Miss Pearlie had finally given in, saying, "If you bound and determined to go to nothin', I can't stop you." Geneva had been beside herself and had plunged with abandon into an emotional vortex, proffering her love and passion like burnt offerings. She closed her eyes to Miss Pearlie's disapproving looks and reveled in the heat and motion of her new life.

And then he left her.

There had been no warning. He dropped her off one day at her house and didn't come back. Weeks passed, and when she could bear her hurt and confusion no longer, she put aside her pride and sought him out. He told her matter-of-factly that he wanted to "start steppin' out again." That was seven weeks ago, and Geneva had heard last Sunday that he had taken up with Lula Raimey, a women at least ten years his senior who was buying him clothes and putting gas in his car. Geneva had tried to put him out of her mind, had tried to pray—but she was consumed with shame and hatred by the way he had thrown her aside. And now she burned with a different passion.

When she had crossed the open field, she could see Miss Zenobia's house at the bottom of the hill where people who ate red clay came to collect it. There was no other house within fifty yards of Miss Zenobia's, and her small hut seemed eerily isolated in the July dawn. Geneva stood for a minute, then crossed over the hill, descended, and walked up the broken steps to Miss Zenobia's front door. She knocked lightly and waited. Hearing no sound, she knocked again, a little louder.

In the distance she could hear mongrel dogs barking. This time Miss Zenobia answered.

"Who is it?"

"It's Geneva Pickens, Miss Zenobia."

"Geneva?"

"Yes ma'am."

"Just a minute."

Geneva waited nervously, hoping Miss Zenobia would hurry. Finally the door opened, and Miss Zenobia stood here in a threadbare blue housecoat.

"What's the matter, chile? Somebody sick?"

"No ma'am."

"Dead?"

"No ma'am. Miss Zenobia, I need to talk to you please ma'am." Miss Zenobia looked at Geneva warily but not unkindly.

"Come on in. Ain't it mighty early for a visit?"

Geneva didn't answer but walked inside and tried to collect herself while Miss Zenobia fiddled with one of the broken steps before closing the front door. When the old woman turned to face Geneva, the girl began with a rush of words: "Miss Zenobia, I hate to bother you so early in the morning but I got a problem and I need some help. I had it in my mind to come before now but I just ain't had the nerve. I don't even know if you can help me—"

"Slow down, chile," Miss Zenobia interrupted. "Set down in this chair and tell me 'bout your trouble."

Geneva sat down in the rocking chair in front of the fireplace, and Miss Zenobia sat on the bed. Geneva glanced around her at the interior of Miss Zenobia's house. It was a one-room house, with a bed, a cedar chest, a tiny kitchen table that held a kerosene lamp, two straight-back chairs, a rocking chair, and a small cupboard. A large iron cooking pot hung over the fireplace in the center of the back wall. The mantel above the fireplace held all manner of bric-a-brac—candy dishes filled with pennies, empty perfume bottles, knitting needles, a paper fan from the funeral home, and an old picture of a smiling, mischievous boy—naked except for the bow and arrows on his arm. On one end of the mantelpiece rested Miss Zenobia's Bible. The head of the bed was to the left of the mantel, and at the foot of the bed her quilts were stacked so high that they almost touched the ceiling. In the right back corner she kept her mop and broom.

Geneva suddenly realized that she had never been inside Miss Zenobia's house—she had only been to the front door. Miss Zenobia was a midwife and could not number the women she had attended. And it was whispered that if a girl missed her time, Miss Zenobia could give her something to bring it on. She had no husband or children and lived alone. Geneva had heard somewhere, perhaps from her Aunt Pearl, that Miss Zenobia had had a husband years ago—she was now in her eighties—but that he had died. Despite her lack of family, everybody—young and old, saint and sinner alike—respected her, and no one crossed her, for it was said that Miss Zenobia was born with a veil and knew things.

"Now," Miss Zenobia began, "is you pregnant?"

"No ma'am. It ain't that." Geneva dropped her head. She felt exposed, for she had sobbed with relief last month when her period had come.

"Well, what is it?"

Geneva swallowed and summoned all the courage she possessed.

"I need a spell Ms. Zenobia."

"A which?"

"A spell. I want to hurt somebody that hurt me."

Miss Zenobia's face became hard, and her body stiffened as she rose from the bed.

"Look here gal. I'm a Christian woman. I don't fool with no hoodoo."

"Yes ma'am, I know you a Christian, but . . . but I just thought—"

"You thought what?"

"I thought maybe—"

"You been listenin' to lyin' niggas what ain't got nothin' better to do than tend to other folks' business. What would Pearlie say if I was to tell her why you come to see me?"

At this, Geneva became agitated.

"Please don't tell Ain' Pearl Miss Zenobia. Please don't tell her why I come."

"Well now I don't know. Pearlie been tryin' her best to raise you up right and here you is, comin' in my house askin' me for a spell. You got religion ain't you?"

"Yes ma'am."

"How long you had religion?"

"Since I was twelve years old."

"Well, you need to go home and pray, cause your feets is slippin' back down in the miry clay. You ought to be shame a yourself, disgracin' your ainey this-a-way."

Geneva began to cry.

"That's right. You need to cry."

Miss Zenobia waited a few moments for Geneva's tears to subside and for her to find her voice.

"Beg pardon Miss Zenobia. Just please don't tell Ain' Pearl."

"I'll study on it," Miss Zenobia said. Then, in a different tone, she said, "But tell me this? Who is it you want to fix?"

"It don't matter."

"Well, since you done broke my rest this mornin', you might as well tell who the cause of it."

Geneva hesitated, then said, "John Allen, John Allen Hutcherson."

"He your boyfriend?"

"No ma'am, not now. He used to be. For a while."

"They tell *me* Lula Raimey done tracked him down."

"Yes ma'am, that's what I heard."

"Well honey, you probably ain't lost nothin' there.

"Yes ma'am."

"But how come you want to fix him?"

Geneva looked down at her hands resting in her lap.

"He didn't do me right."

Needing no further explanation, Miss Zenobia said, matter-of-factly, "Well, you ain't the first woman been wronged by a man. Mens is like that—most of 'em anyhow." Geneva looked up at Miss Zenobia.

"Was your husband a good man?"

"He was a whole lot better'n some I guess. Chile, can't nobody tell me nothin' bout no man I don't already know. Some mens would tell a lie for credit when they payin' cash for the truth. But we all got to give an account one day."

"Well I guess I better be goin'. I'd appreciate it Miss Zenobia if you wouldn't tell Ain' Pearl."

"Like I told you, chile, I'll study on it."

Geneva straightened her head scarf and bent over to tie her shoelaces that had come undone. When Miss Zenobia looked down at the bent figure of the girl, the dejection of her bowed head, the weary motions of her hands, the old woman felt a sudden rush of tenderness and old memories. She thought of her sister Annie, who had run off at fourteen to get married.

Annie had died of tuberculosis at age twenty in their mother's house. She also thought of the turbulence of her own youth, for Miss Zenobia had not always been a Christian. And she remembered the time her mother had whipped her for singing "devil music" on Sunday. The whipping had made large welts on her arms and legs, but she had never forgotten the song:

Your time now, papa,
Be mine some old day.

When Geneva stood up, Miss Zenobia said, "Listen. If I was to tell you sump'm, could you keep it?"

"Yes ma'am."

"Set down."

Geneva sat in the rocker, and Miss Zenobia resumed her seat on the bed. When she began, her voice was strong and rhythmic, explaining to Geneva in careful detail what to do. When she was done, she stood up.

Geneva had listened intently to every word, mesmerized. When she rose to leave, she said, "How much I owe you Miss Zenobia?" Miss Zenobia thought for a second, then said, "Just bring me a basket of figs from your Ain' Pearlie's tree."

Geneva walked back the same way she had come, but half way home—for some reason—she became suddenly fearful and quickened her pace. When she reached her back yard, her aunt was feeding the chickens.

"Chile, where you been this early in the morning?

"The cow got out."

"Again?"

"I got up first light to go to the toilet, and I saw she was out."

"Did you catch her?"

"Uh huh."

"You better go over today and tell your Uncle Bud I need him to fix that fence."

The next day Geneva found a bushel basket, filled it with as many figs as she could pick in one gathering, and left the basket at Miss Zenobia's front steps.

Geneva did not act right away on what Miss Zenobia had told her. For one thing, she began to have misgivings. Miss Zenobia did not say exactly what would happen to John Allen, so Geneva did not know what to expect. Would all of his hair fall out? Would someone steal his car? Would he be laid off? Something worse? And whatever happened, Geneva wondered, "Won't I go to hell." Then she thought of Miss Zenobia, who was a Christian woman—everybody knew that—and if Miss Zenobia thought it was all right, well, it was probably not such a serious sin.

But there was another problem. The ingredients Miss Zenobia had spoken of as part of the "fixing" were fairly common household items—all except one. She had said that Geneva had to have a piece of John Allen's clothing. So she waited.

One afternoon, as she was returning home from her Uncle Bud's, she passed through the field in back of John Allen's house and saw, from about 50 yards away, Miss Hutcherson's wash hanging on the clothesline. Geneva knew that, despite his relationship with Lula Raimey, John Allen still lived with his mother. She crossed the field and saw that John Allen's car was gone. The house looked quiet, and she supposed that Miss Hutcherson and her girls had gone to town—it was Saturday. Geneva entered the back yard, went up to the door and knocked. When she was certain that no one was home, she walked back to the clothesline, took down a pair of men's socks, and stuffed them into her dress pocket.

Now she was ready.

One night, after Miss Pearlie had gone to sleep, Geneva performed the ritual, just as Miss Zenobia had instructed.

She had forgotten to ask Miss Zenobia how soon the spell would take effect, and she was surprised, two weeks later, to see John Allen walking out of Carter's Grocery laughing with a boy named Jake. He sure seemed all right—more than all right. Geneva eavesdropped on all Miss Pearlie's visitors to find out if any of them had news of John Allen's troubles, but she could hear nothing.

Summer faded into autumn, and still there was no sign. One morning, as Geneva was milking the cow, she had a horrible thought. Suppose the socks she had stolen did not belong to John Allen. He was the only boy in the family, and his mother had no husband. But John Allen's mother was loose—each of her four children had been fathered by a different man. Suppose the socks had belonged to one of her men friends. Geneva recoiled at the thought of some man being "fixed" because she had made a mistake.

Months passed and winter came. By this time Geneva had begun to doubt, and the entire episode took on an aura of fantasy. Sometimes she wondered whether she had ever gone to visit Miss Zenobia, or whether it had all been a dream. Whenever she saw Miss Zenobia, the old woman behaved as if nothing had happened. She inquired after Miss Pearlie, talked of church happenings and the weather, and complained of dizzy spells, calling them "swimmin' in the head." She never acknowledged the basket of figs.

It was an unusually cold winter. People stayed inside whenever possible, and visits were infrequent. Neighbors saw one another primarily in church or in town on Saturdays. Geneva's legs were burned from standing long periods in front of the fireplace, and Miss Pearl caught a bad cold and coughed for almost a month. The confinement of winter was nerve-racking, but the frigid temperatures were the only out-of-the-ordinary occurrence in the predictable routine of their lives. And as far as Geneva knew, nothing had happened to John Allen.

When April brought warm days and cool, comfortable nights, Geneva had lost faith completely and stopped thinking about the spell. Almost imperceptibly the pain of John Allen's betrayal had faded, and she began to tolerate Cecil Cooley. Miss Pearlie threw up her hands and decided that Geneva had no sense at all—everybody knew that insanity ran in the Cooley family, and, besides, Cecil was cross-eyed.

Miss Pearl did not need to worry. After a few weeks Geneva stopped seeing Cecil and started singing in the church choir. She even took to shouting out loud like the older women, and folks said it was "upliftin'" to see somebody that young so filled with the spirit. She had also caught the eye of a young church deacon who had a steady job and was from a good family. Her heart did not quiver when she thought of him or when she heard his name called, but she appreciated him, and he seemed overly fond of her. Miss Pearlie was overjoyed that her child was "back on the right path," and life between the two women was easier.

One evening in late September—nine days after Miss Zenobia's funeral—John Allen's car was hit by a pick-up truck. He was paralyzed from the waist down, and the doctors said he might never walk again. Months later, after he came home from the hospital, Geneva brought him sweetbread, and some figs from her Aunt Pearlie's tree.

Nothing Very New

It was a nice funeral. The small frame church was filled to capacity, with some people standing in the back and along the windows on each side. The service wasn't long, which was a blessing in view of the ninety-degree heat that had already wilted some of the lilies and chrysanthemums framing the casket. From the back of the church it looked as if every man and woman had a paper fan from the funeral home, waving it back and forth in a nearly futile effort to raise a breeze. Only the children seemed not to mind the stifling air.

The eulogy was brief. The choir sang "Jesus Keep Me near the Cross" and "Rock of Ages" with some restraint, and the hymns sounded sad because of the occasion and not the way they were sung. The family and close friends wept quietly until the time came for viewing the body. Then they broke, but that was to be expected. The girl—Virginia—wailed inconsolably and almost collapsed as she was led back to her seat. The husband, too, seemed doubled over with grief.

The woman who had died was Juanita Wilkerson—Nita to everybody who knew her. She had endured a heart condition for almost ten years, sometimes going to the hospital for some complication but mostly just staying home. She was not totally bedridden, until the very end, and she was able to perform light household chores. But except for visits to the doctor and infrequent trips to town, she was confined to her house. She had felt well enough to attend church only four or five times in the last five years.

Nita married Oscar Wilkerson when she was sixteen and bore a child, Mattie Ruth, a year later. When Mattie Ruth was eighteen, she gave birth to a baby girl, Virginia, and before the child reached her second birthday, Mattie Ruth—still unmarried—moved to Memphis, leaving Virginia to be raised by Nita and Oscar. The baby's father had joined the army a month after she was born and was never heard from again. Virginia was now a young woman of nineteen, and all her life, Nita and Oscar had been "Mama" and "Daddy."

Mattie Ruth was killed in an automobile accident barely two years before Nita's death, and many concluded that the daughter's passing was just too much for Nita's weak heart.

After the service inside the church was over, they carried Nita's casket down the middle aisle, out of the church, and around the back to the graveyard. The grass has been recently cut, but there were still plenty of weeds and anthills. As the family gathered around the coffin, the minister uttered the last words, ending with the benediction, and the funeral was over.

As mourners were leaving the church ground, Miss Cora Griffin voiced a sentiment shared by not a few others: "First Mattie Ruth and now Nita. Lord, help Virginia and poor Oscar?" The two or three other women who heard her responded with humming noises in their throats that needed no translation. Oscar could be seen walking stoop-shouldered away from the grave, flanked by his brothers and cousins, after Nita had been lowered into the ground. He had not cried out during the funeral service but had wept bitterly, similar to the way he usually wept during regular church service. In fact, his crying was such a regular occurrence in church that some of the older children from Sunday school nicknamed him "Weeping Wilkerson." Whether the sermon was fiery or dry, the singing of the choir inspired or flat, Oscar could be counted on to shed tears. He would sit in his spot in the men's amen corner, his head buried in his large white handkerchief, and weep as though his heart was aching with a pain too tender to touch.

Oscar was a devoted church member—a deacon—and he hardly ever missed a church meeting unless he was very ill. At one time, though, he was known as a rounder and someone who liked the ladies. Years ago, so one unpleasant rumor went, he had deliberately shot Clark Reese in the leg while the two of them were out hunting—shot him and claimed it was an accident. It was said that Oscar and Clark were seeing the same woman. No one really believed that Oscar shot Clark on purpose—the wound was slight—but it made a good story. There were other stories about Oscar—though not quite as dramatic—but all that was long passed. Since his marriage to Nita, he had been a model of rectitude and not at all averse to pointing out the errors of others. Still, some uncharitable folk wondered whether he wept in church not out of piety or being spirit-filled but because of past sins.

There was one thing about Oscar, however, that no one could dispute. He had always had an outsized affection for Virginia. From the time she was born, she had been a balm for his tired heart. Virginia was a good girl growing up, but because of Oscar's indulgence, she had never been afraid to talk back to him or exhibit behavior that other parents and grandparents would have considered disrespectful. From time to time, when she was still a child, Oscar tried to put his foot down, usually over some trifle. And Virginia would obey him, insolently, after speaking her mind. Oscar shrank from her angry words and always felt a little defeated after these encounters. He knew he was a fraud, and she always got her way in the end. Virginia, for her part, loved Oscar and at the same time was slightly contemptuous of him. She saw through his blustering to the weakness that lay underneath, and she could not pity him.

It was to Nita that the girl gave her true devotion. From age eleven, because of Nita's health, Virginia had assumed most of the housekeeping duties, and she never complained. Being forced to take on adult responsibility so early had fostered a marked independence in her. She was a friendly, good-natured, popular girl who was tall and angular and who liked playing basketball and softball in high school. But she was no follower of crowds. She had many acquaintances who were fond of her but few close friends. Oscar's pay at the sawmill did not provide many luxuries, and her clothes sometimes came from Mr. Bruce, a white man who came through several times a year selling merchandise from his truck. The family had never owned a car and had to catch rides to town and to the doctor, but Virginia held her head as high as anyone else and somewhat higher than some. To Nita she was always the caring, dutiful child, and the older woman was genuinely grateful. With Mattie Ruth gone and her sisters living in other places, without Virginia Nita would have had no close female relative nearby. And she needed another woman. Only another woman knew how to help you in and out of bed or onto the bedpan when needed. Only another female knew how to sit beside the bed and say nothing, just sit there, sharing the quiet and loneliness of the sick room. Nita and Virginia were always gentle with each other, speaking softly, treading lightly, as if the bond of understanding they shared was too sacred for loud or vulgar display.

After Nita's service, back at Oscar's house there was the usual after-funeral gathering. People filled their plates with fried chicken, ham, macaroni and cheese, black-eyed peas, collard greens, and a variety of cakes and pies. The house contained no alcohol but plenty of Coca Cola, Pepsi, and ice water. Neighbors and friends continued to bring food and drink throughout the afternoon and evening, and it was after ten o'clock before the house was left to the family. Oscar's brother from Cincinnati and Nita's sister Carrie and her husband from Atlanta left two days later, leaving Oscar and Virginia alone.

There were things to be done—accounts to be settled, thank-you notes and letters to be sent. But after a while, all that business was completed, and with no common tasks to occupy them, Oscar and Virginia found themselves abashed in each other's presence, an entirely alien and utterly frightening feeling. They got up each day, washed, and got dressed, and went through the motions of polite cohabitation. However, without Nita, things were off balance, disordered. Instead of their usual easy familiarity, Oscar and Virginia were guarded with each other, their conversation measured and deliberate. Each was vaguely aware that with Nita gone some element necessary for their coexistence was irrevocably altered. Had a veil been torn that could not be mended, or had a curtain descended that could not be pushed aside?

Virginia had trouble sleeping. She thought of her mother, Mattie Ruth, whom she had never really gotten to know, in spite of trips to Memphis—one every year or so—to see her. Virginia would catch the bus, stay for a week, and come back feeling as if she had visited a cousin. After leaving Virginia to Nita and Oscar when the child was barely two, Mattie Ruth had seldom returned home. She came for family funerals, and once when Nita was in the hospital, and occasionally at Christmas, but she was a stranger to the town and felt easy only with Nita and Oscar. As she grew older, she yearned for a closer relationship with Virginia but settled for what she had.

When she died, Virginia and Oscar traveled to Memphis in a borrowed car to take care of the funeral arrangements, Nita being too frail for the journey. As Virginia lay on her back looking up at the wooden beams of her bedroom ceiling, she cried noiselessly for Nita and tried to recall what Mattie Ruth's eyes looked like.

One day, about three months after Nita's death, Virginia got a call from her Aunt Carrie at Miss Alice's house next door. Later that day she caught a ride to town with Mrs. Frazier, the preacher's wife, and bought a new skirt and blouse with money she had saved from condolence gifts. When she returned home, Oscar was sitting at the kitchen table drinking coffee.

"I'm leaving, Daddy," she said.

"Leaving? Where you going?"

"I'm going to stay with Aunt Carrie. She says she'll try to help me get into college."

"You ain't said nothing to me."

"I've made up my mind."

"Carrie didn't say nothing to me when she was here."

"She wanted to wait awhile."

"You better think about this thing. You can't just hop up and move somewhere, just like that."

"I've thought about it. I was going to wait until after Christmas, but when she called today, she said maybe she could get me a job working at the hospital where she works. So I'm leaving tomorrow."

Oscar was silent. He stared in front of him as if he hadn't heard her. Virginia put her things away and started preparing dinner. Neither of them spoke. Later, when they were eating, Oscar said, "I hope you know what you're doing, that's all." She answered, "It'll be good for me to get away. It's time." Both ate slowly as though they wanted to prolong the meal, but in fact, Virginia desperately wanted it to end. In her mind she was already on the bus to Atlanta. Aunt Carrie's invitation was a gift from heaven. She was eager to be away from this house, this place and its people. The past was a burden she longed to throw off.

When the dinner was mercifully over and the dishes washed and put away, Virginia started getting her things together. Midway through her packing, Oscar came to the door of her bedroom and watched her for a moment or two. Finally he spoke. "Life is hard, Virginia. I did the best I could." Virginia didn't answer but continued putting her belongings into a large, brown, somewhat worn suitcase. She knew that if she spoke to his words her voice would tremble, and she could not afford to weaken or to comfort him now. So she said flatly, "Maybe you can have a telephone put in—that would be good." Oscar stood in the doorway for a moment longer before saying, "Maybe I will," and retreated to his room. He took out his Bible and turned to the book of Proverbs, reading slowly.

After she had finished packing, even though it was only 9:30, Virginia went to bed. Mrs. Frazier was picking her up early the next morning to catch the 7:20 bus. When Oscar had finished reading his Bible, he came to her bedroom door, which was closed, and called her name, but she couldn't hear him. For the first time in weeks, she was soundly sleeping.

The next morning Mrs. Frazier blew her horn promptly at six. Virginia and Oscar walked to the car, he put her brown suitcase in the back seat, and Virginia got in. She told Oscar that she would write.

After the car had disappeared down the road, Oscar walked around the house to the backyard among the plum trees. It was Saturday, and he did not have to go to work. A slight morning breeze stirred, and a blue jay flew high over his head. He began to weep as he looked up at the purple sky that promised rain. He hoped he would get a letter from Virginia soon, and suddenly he remembered the yellow hat Mattie Ruth wore seventeen years ago when she caught the train to Memphis. But mostly he thought of Nita, finally at peace—Nita, whose price was far above rubies.

Printed in the United States
By Bookmasters